STORYBOOK SKILLS

STORYBOOK CONCEPTS

by Marilynn G. Barr

Publisher: Roberta Suid

Production: Little Acorn & Associates, Inc.

MM2206
STORYBOOK CONCEPTS
Entire contents copyright © 2005
by Monday Morning Books, Inc.

For a complete catalog, write to the address below:
Monday Morning Books, Inc.
PO Box 1134
Inverness, CA 94937

Call our toll-free number: 1-800-255-6049
E-mail us at: MMBooks@aol.com
Visit our Web site:
http://www.mondaymorningbooks.com
For more products featuring art by Marilynn G. Barr visit www.littleacornbooks.com

Monday Morning is a registered trademark of
Monday Morning Books, Inc.

ISBN 1-57612-258-1

Printed in the United States of America
9 8 7 6 5 4 3 2 1

Storybook Concepts

Contents

Introduction

Storybook Concepts is one of four books in the Storybook Skills series. The hands-on activities in this book help children master concepts. Hands-on activities focus on ideas such as up and down, right and left, hot and cold, near and far, and many other concepts that are often difficult for small children.

Based on favorite children's books such as *Curious George*, rhymes such as "Ladybug Ladybug," and fables such as "The Little Red Hen," the activities in Storybook Concepts come alive to children's imaginations. Whether they are differentiating between big and little, sorting different-sized birthday gifts, or learning map-reading skills in "Mr. Monkey Goes to Town," children will be engaged in skill-building practice.

Activities in this book may enrich other storybooks, as well as the ones featured here. Play the "Fly Away Home" game after reading *The Grouchy Ladybug* or create a "Big Picture for Big Dog" after reading *Pinkerton, Behave!*

Patterns in this book may also be used in a variety of ways, including making stick puppets or other art projects, or as decorations for the classroom. Below are simple designs to program cutouts for additional matching activities.

Storybook Concepts provides a wide range of concept-enhancing projects.

Pattern Designs

Matching Big and Little

Reproduce, color, laminate, and cut out big and little dogs, bones, bowls, toys, and houses. Decorate and write "Matching Big and Little" on the front of a large envelope. Children can work individually or in small groups to practice sorting and matching big and little. Option: Cut out and laminate assorted big and little geometric shapes for children to sort and match.

Happy Birthday, Big Dog

Reproduce big dog and gift patterns for children to sort big and little. Provide each child with a folder and an envelope. Have children color and cut out their patterns. Then have them decorate and glue their big dog cutouts to the fronts of their folders. Write "Happy Birthday, Big Dog" on the front and "big" and "little" on the inside of each child's folder. Help each child glue an envelope to the back of his or her folder to store gifts.

A Big Picture for Big Dog

Prepare a work station with large sheets of construction paper, crayons, markers, scissors, glue, and big dog patterns for children to create big dog art. Have children choose, color, and cut out patterns. Help each child arrange and glue their patterns on a sheet of construction paper. Cut a sheet of wrapping paper larger than the construction paper for each child. Glue each picture in the center of a wrapping paper frame. Laminate and mount on a bulletin board entitled "Our Big Dog Gallery." Option: Make "Little Pictures" for little dogs.

Big Dog's Little Dog Bed

Provide each child with a folder to decorate and write "Big Dog's Little Dog Bed" on the front. Reproduce a big dog and little toy patterns for each child to color and cut out. Have children glue their big dogs and beds inside the folders. Then have them glue their little toy cutouts on the beds. Invite children to use their folders to tell a story about big dog's little toys.

Big Dog and Ball

Provide children with craft sticks, crayons, markers, scissors, and glue to make stick puppets.

Big Dog Things

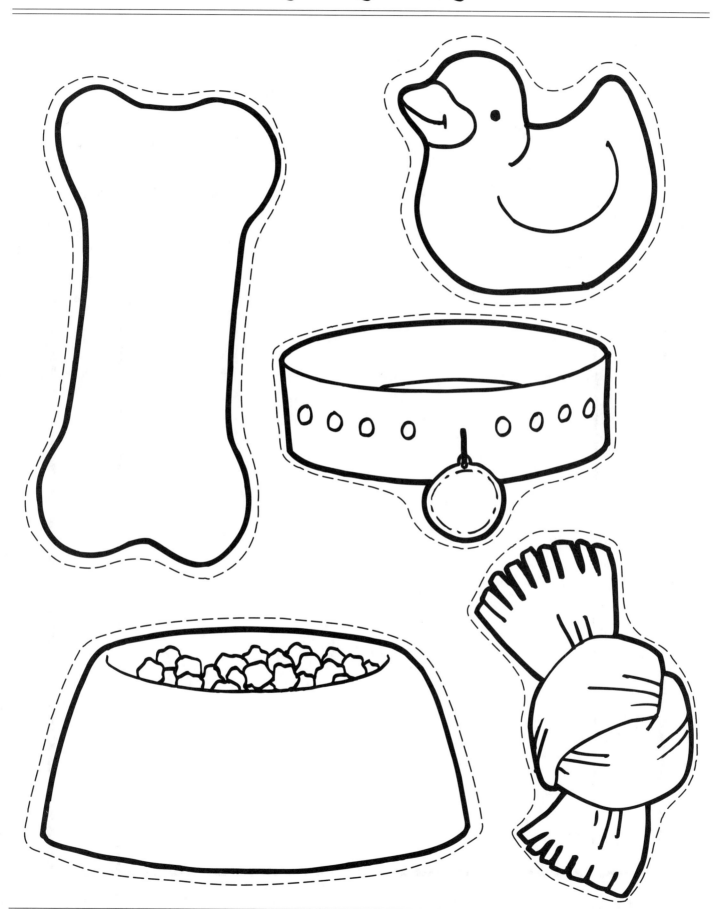

Big Dog House

Children can put all of big dog's things in big dog's house.

Little Dog and Little Dog Things

Provide children with craft sticks, crayons, markers, scissors, and glue to make stick puppets.

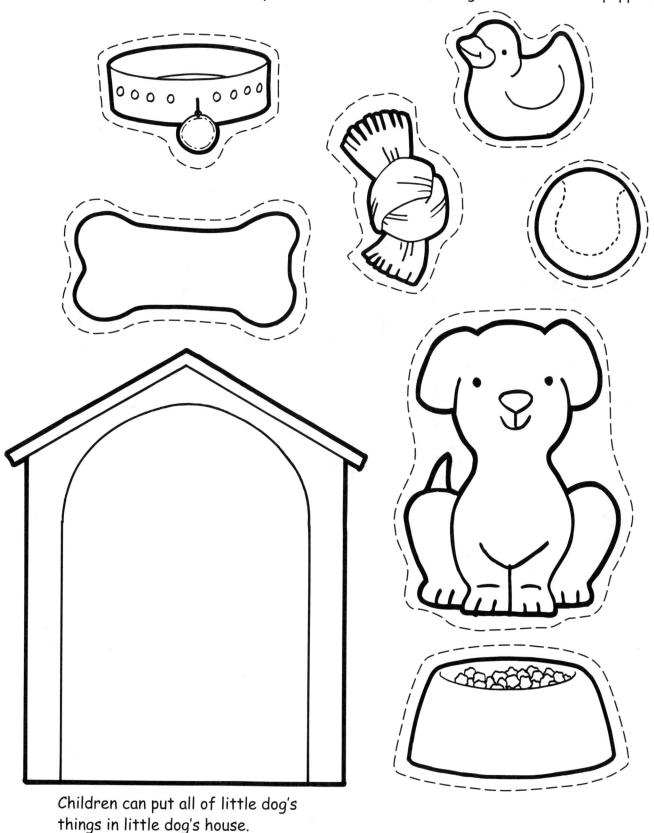

Children can put all of little dog's
things in little dog's house.

Big Dog's Birthday Gifts and Bed

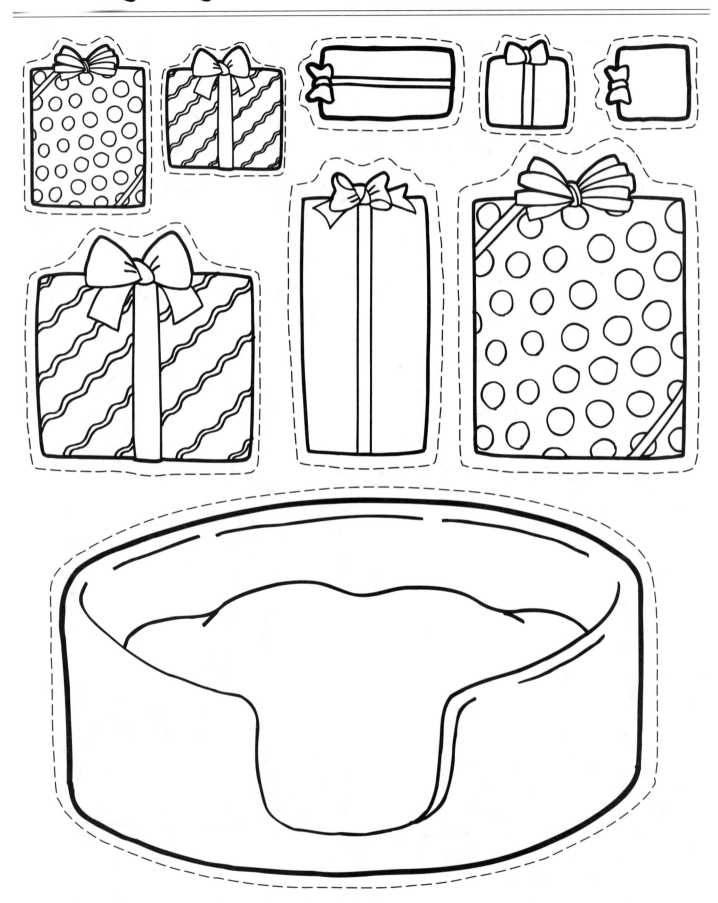

Let's Play Who's Got the Big Dog?

Assembly

Reproduce and color four sets of "Who's Got the Big Dog?" game cards. Glue a sheet of wrapping paper to the back of each page of cards. Laminate and cut apart the cards. Note: You will need only one "Big Dog" card. Discard extra "Big Dog" cards. Decorate and write "Who's Got the Big Dog?" on the front of an envelope to store the cards.

To Play

Up to four players can play. Shuffle and deal a card to each player until all but one card is dealt. Place the last card, face up, on the table. If this card is the "Big Dog" card, reshuffle, and redeal the cards. Note: The player holding the "Big Dog" does not reveal that he or she has the card. The first player places a matching card face up on top of the card on the table, then the next player takes a turn. If a player doesn't have a card that matches, the player skips his or her turn and the next player takes a turn. However if the player has no match but has the "Big Dog" he or she must play the "Big Dog" card. The "Big Dog" can only be played if the holder has no other matching card. Play ends when the "Big Dog" card is played. Children can also play Concentration or Go Fish or match big and little with the cards.

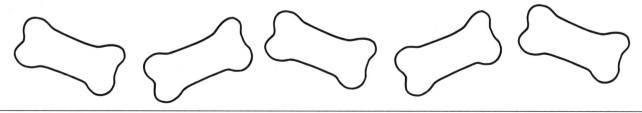

Who's Got the Big Dog? Game Cards

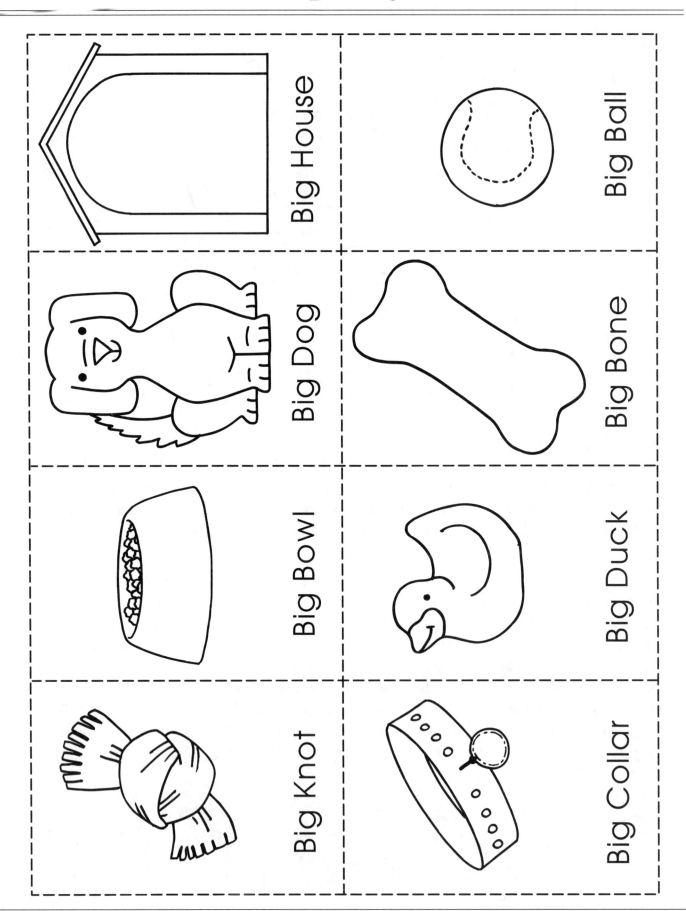

Big House

Big Ball

Big Dog

Big Bone

Big Bowl

Big Duck

Big Knot

Big Collar

12

Who's Got the Big Dog? Game Cards

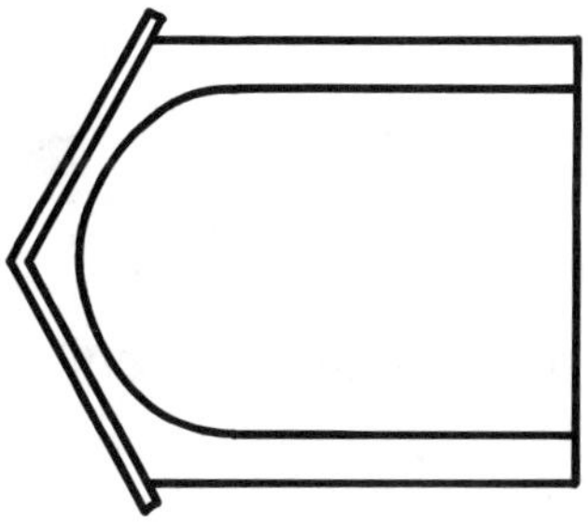

Little House

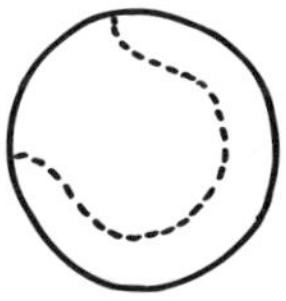

Little Ball

Little Dog

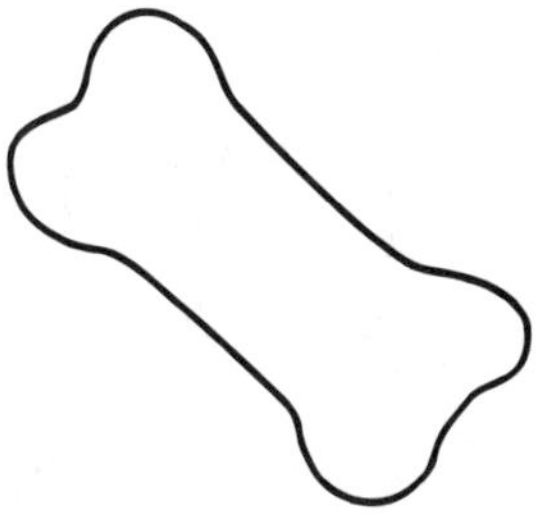

Little Bone

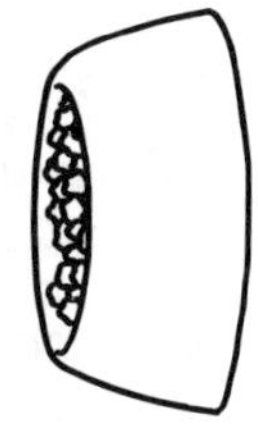

Little Bowl

Little Duck

Little Knot

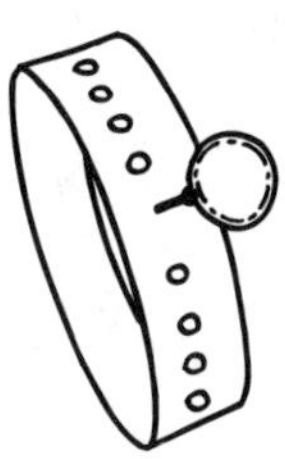

Little Collar

Mr. Monkey Goes to Town

Reproduce a monkey, neighborhood map patterns, and neighborhood cards for each child to color and cut out. Provide a folder for each child to decorate. Write each child's name on the front of his or her folder.

Matching in the center, glue each child's neighborhood map to the inside of his or her folder, then laminate. Children develop spatial concept skills as you give oral instructions to place objects in different locations on their neighborhood maps.

Make children giggle when you give silly instructions such as, "Place a tree in the middle of the pond."

Where is the Bunny?

After reading *Curious George Flies a Kite*, reproduce a bunny pattern for each child to color and cut out. At a table away from the rest of the class, have one child at a time arrange neighborhood cards and the bunny cutout on his or her neighborhood map. Then invite children, in turn, to ask specific spatial questions to guess where the bunny is on the map. Questions can include: Is the bunny on the left side of the street? Is the bunny sitting on the rock? Is the bunny under the tree? Is the bunny in front of the building?

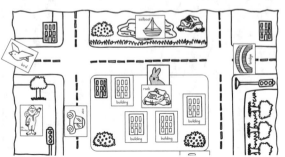

Hats, Hats Everywhere

Children practice sorting hats by size, shape, and design. Reproduce a sheet of hat patterns (p. 19) for children to color. Laminate, then help each child cut out his or her hats. Provide an envelope for children to store their hat cutouts. Have children draw hats or other decorations on the fronts of their envelopes. Write "Hats, Hats Everywhere" and each child's name on his or her envelope. Reproduce colored construction paper hats for children to cut out and sort by color, shape, size, and design.

Mr. Monkey Flies a Kite

Provide each child with a folder to decorate. Write "Mr. Monkey Flies a Kite" on the front of each child's folder. Tape an envelope to the back of each child's folder to store kites and tails. Reproduce a monkey pattern for each child to color, cut out and glue inside his or her folder. Program, then reproduce kites and tails with matching geometric shapes, arrows, sets of stars, or other designs. Children use their folders as a work surface to sort and place tails on matching kites.

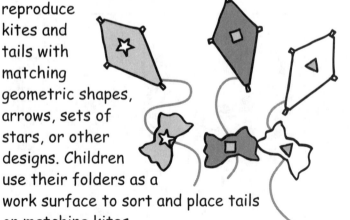

Monkey and Bunnies

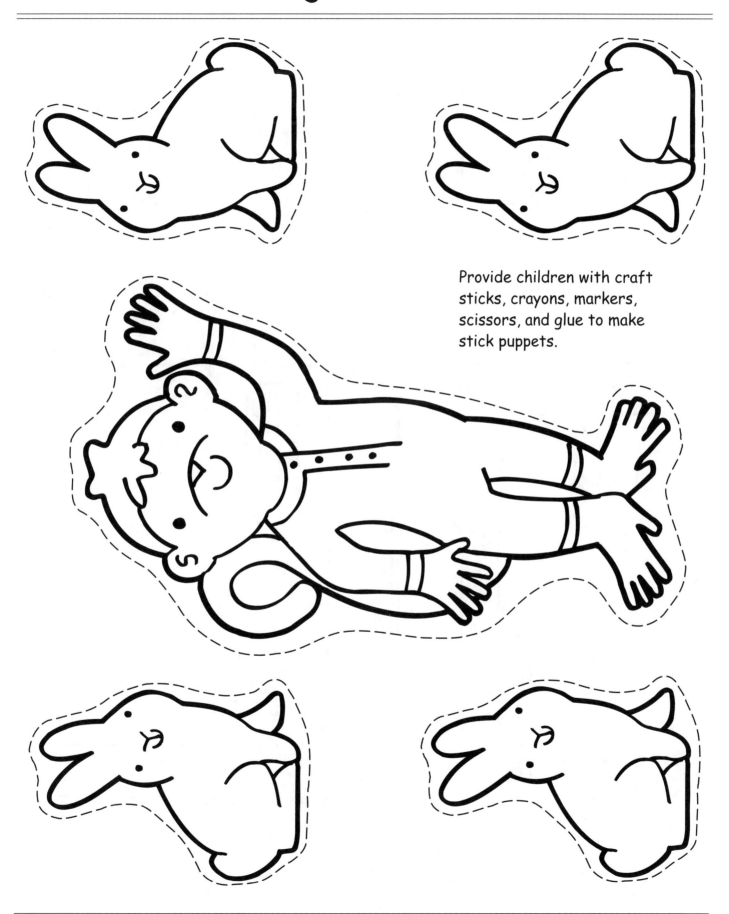

Provide children with craft sticks, crayons, markers, scissors, and glue to make stick puppets.

Neighborhood Map

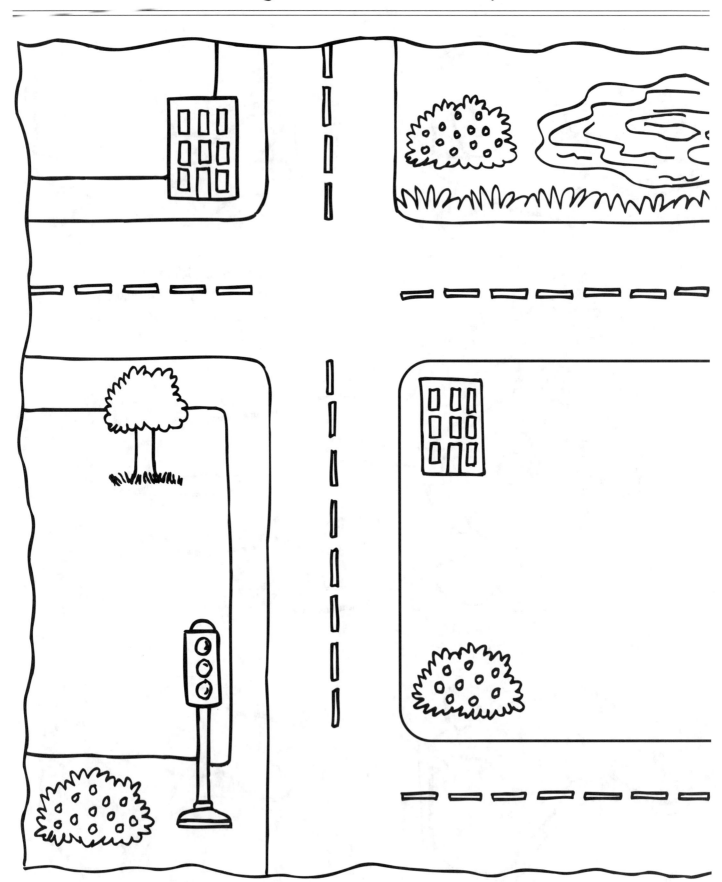

Neighborhood Map

Neigborhood Cards

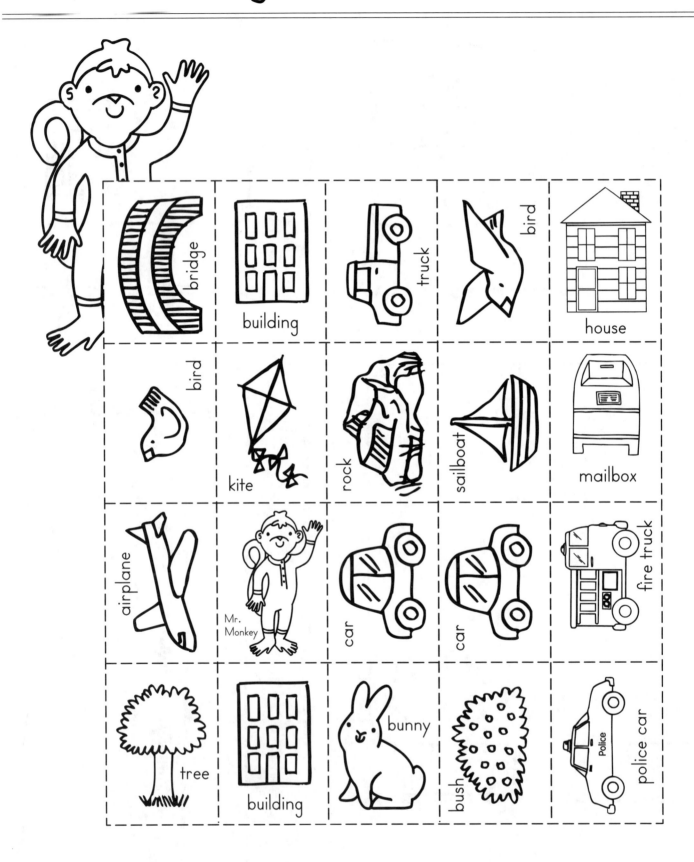

bridge

building

truck

bird

house

bird

kite

rock

sailboat

mailbox

airplane

Mr. Monkey

car

car

fire truck

tree

building

bunny

bush

police car

Hats

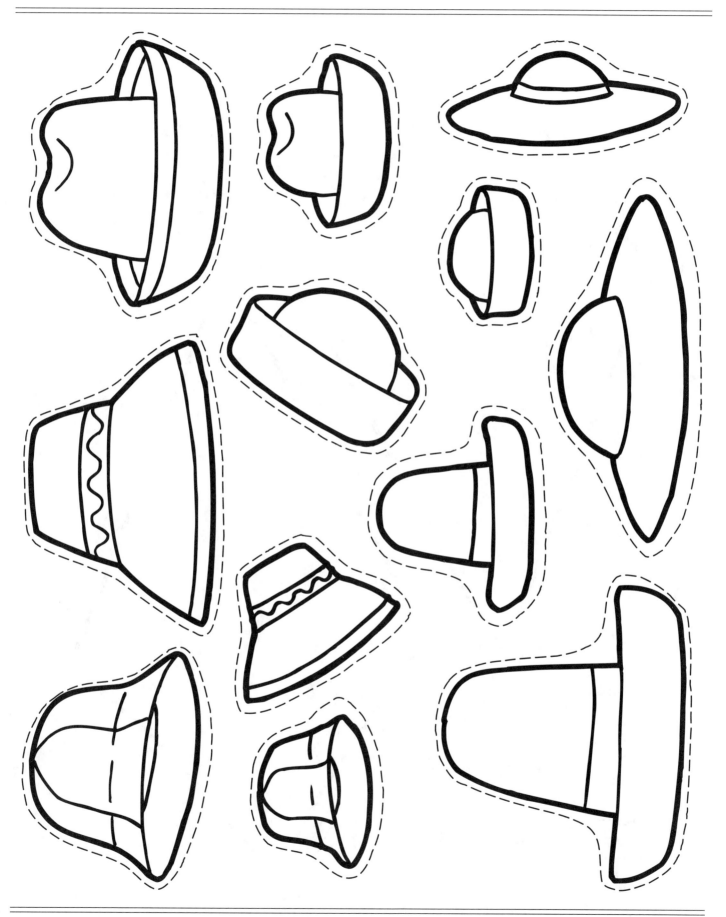

Kites and Tails

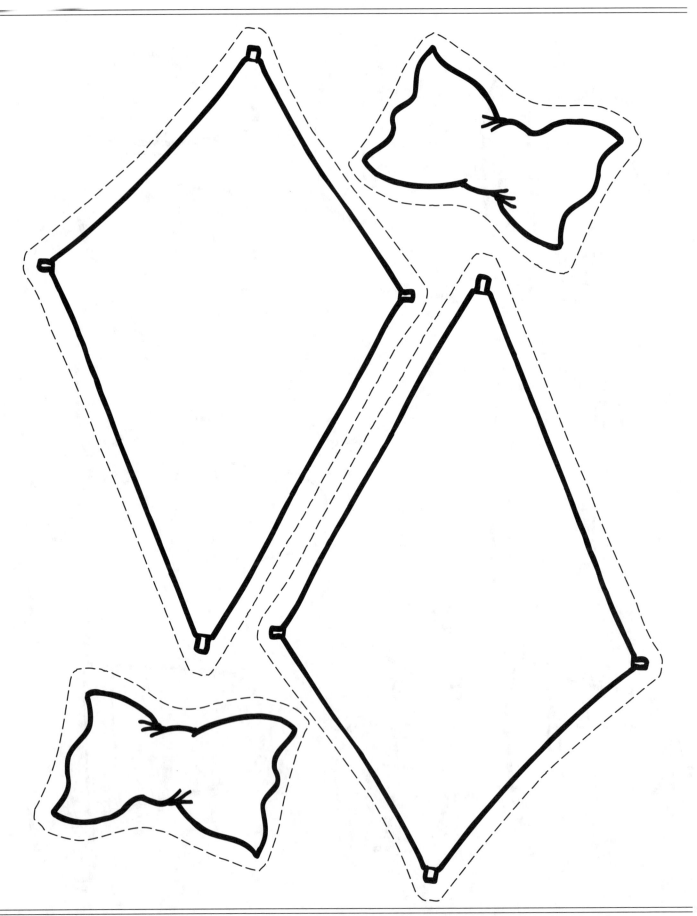

Let's Play *Help the Bunnies Go Home*

Assembly

Reproduce, color, and cut out the "Help the Bunnies Go Home" game board patterns. Matching in the center, glue the game board patterns on a sheet of oak tag. Decorate the border around the game board, then laminate. Reproduce, color, laminate, then cut out the pawns. Tape a small envelope to the back of the game board for pawn storage.

To Play

Set up the game board on a table. Each player, in turn, rolls a die, and moves his or her pawn the matching number of spaces. Play continues until each player reaches The End.

Pawns

Help the Bunnies Go Home Game Board

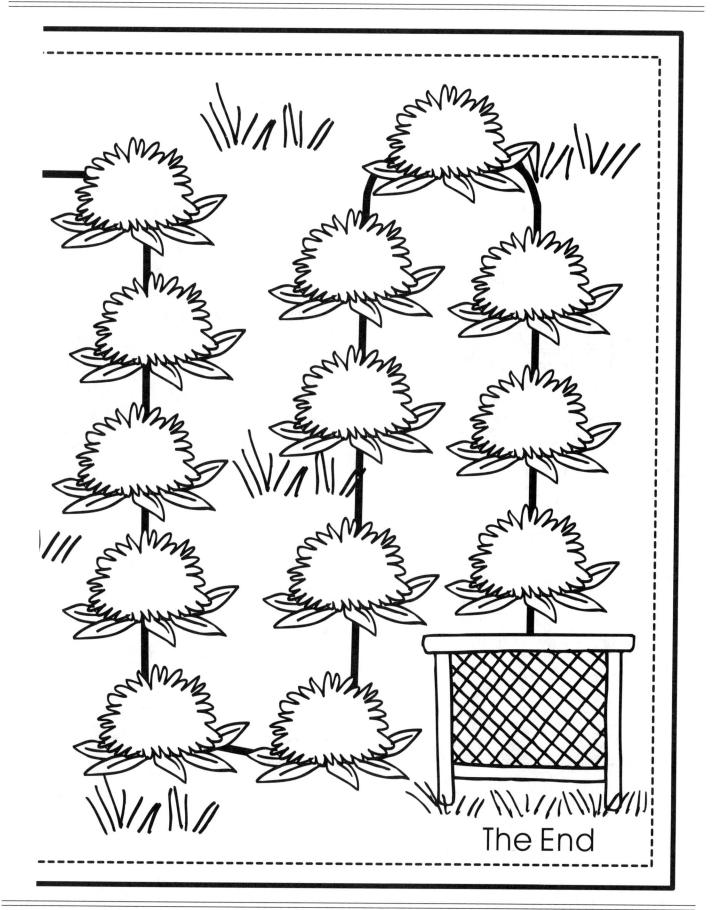

The End

Design a 3-D Cottage

Prepare a work station with cereal Os, pom poms, dry pasta noodles, crayons, markers, scissors, glue, glitter, and oak tag or construction paper. Also provide cottage patterns (p. 26). Have children color, cut out, and glue cottage patterns on oak tag or construction paper. Then have children decorate their cottages with cereal Os, pom poms, dry pasta noodles, and glitter.

Healthy Treat Cottage

Reproduce a cottage pattern and two sets of healthy treat stones for each child to color and cut out. Have each child glue healthy treat stones on his or her cottage, then glue the decorated cottage on a sheet of oak tag. Write children's names on the backs of finished pictures. Mount finished pictures on a display board entitled "Our Healthy Treat Cottages."

A Walk Through the Woods

Provide each child with a folder. Have children draw and color grass and trees on the inside of the folder. Write "A Walk in the Woods" on the front of each child's folder. Then have children decorate the fronts of their folders. Reproduce a set of "A Walk Through the Woods" patterns for children to color and cut out. Help each child glue an envelope to the back of his or her folder to store cutouts. Children practice placing the cutouts in front, behind, next to, under, to the left, and so on, on their open folders as you give oral directions. Examples: *Hansel is standing in front of the bush. Gretel is standing under the bridge.*

Veggie Match

Reproduce, color, laminate, then cut apart two sets of vegetable cards (p. 32). Glue two to four vegetable cards from one set on clean styrofoam vegetable trays. Children practice placing matching vegetable cards on the trays. Store the cards and trays in a large resealable plastic bag.

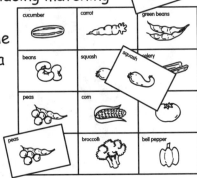

Hansel and Gretel

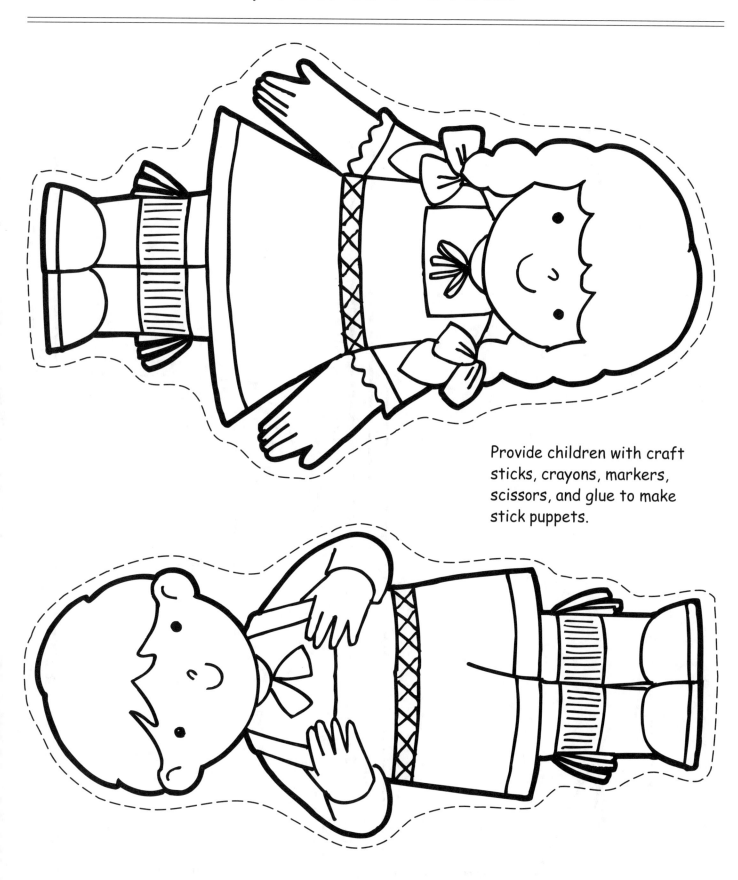

Provide children with craft sticks, crayons, markers, scissors, and glue to make stick puppets.

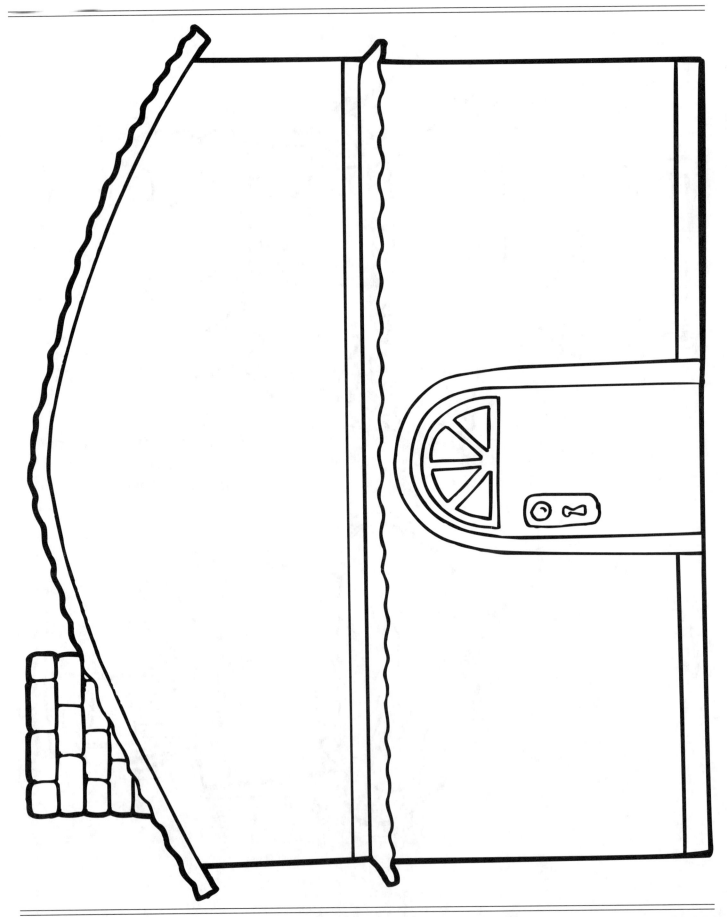

26

Healthy Treat Stones

tomato

apple

bell pepper

watermelon

grapes

cherries

cucumber

strawberry

carrot

celery

cheese

peanut

banana

radish

broccoli

A Walk Through the Woods Patterns

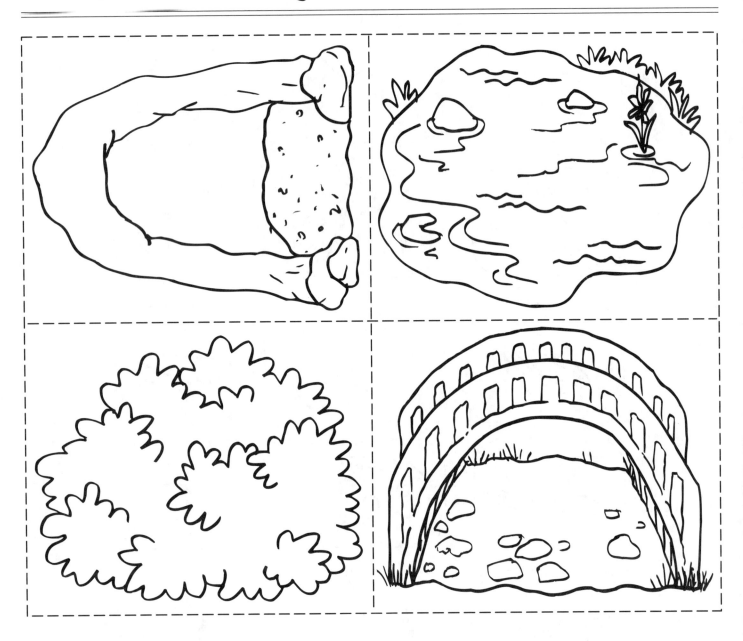

Let's Play *Follow the Veggie Path*

Assembly

Reproduce, color, and cut out the "Follow the Veggie Path" game board patterns. Overlap and match the game board halves at the center. Glue the game board patterns on a sheet of oak tag. Decorate the border around the game board, then laminate. Reproduce, color, laminate, then cut out the pawns and two sets of game cards. Measure, cut, and tape a construction paper pocket to the back of the game board for pawn and game card storage.

To Play

Set up the game board on a table. Shuffle and place the game cards, face down, next to the game board. Each player, in turn, draws a card and moves his or her pawn to the space with the matching vegetable. Players place used cards in a discard pile. When all cards have been drawn, reshuffle the discard pile for children to continue playing. Play continues until each player reaches The End.

Pawns

Follow the Veggie Path Game Board

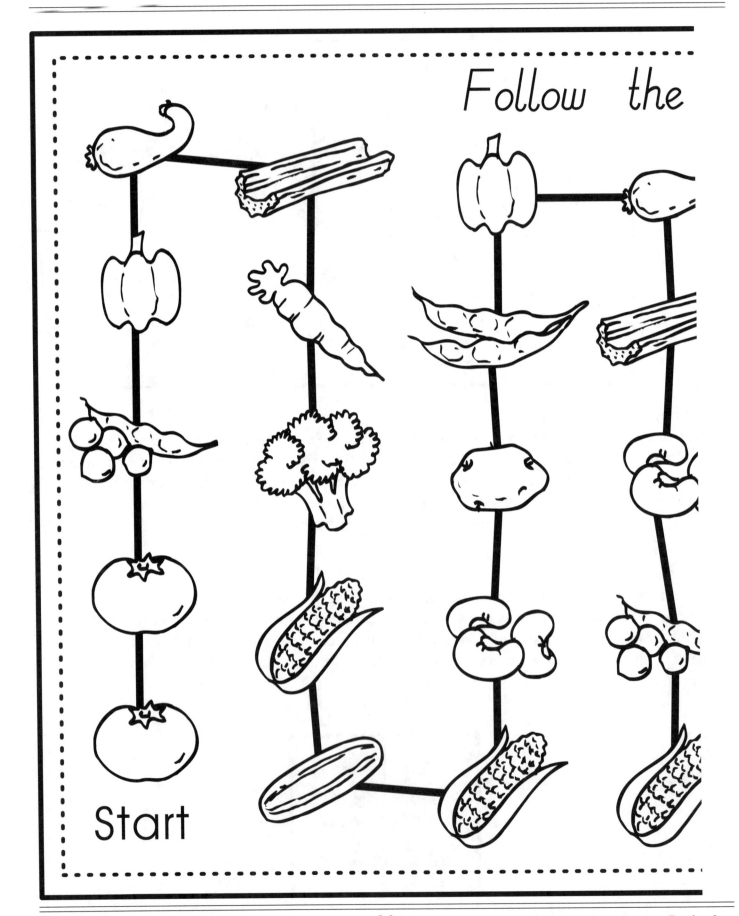

Follow the

Start

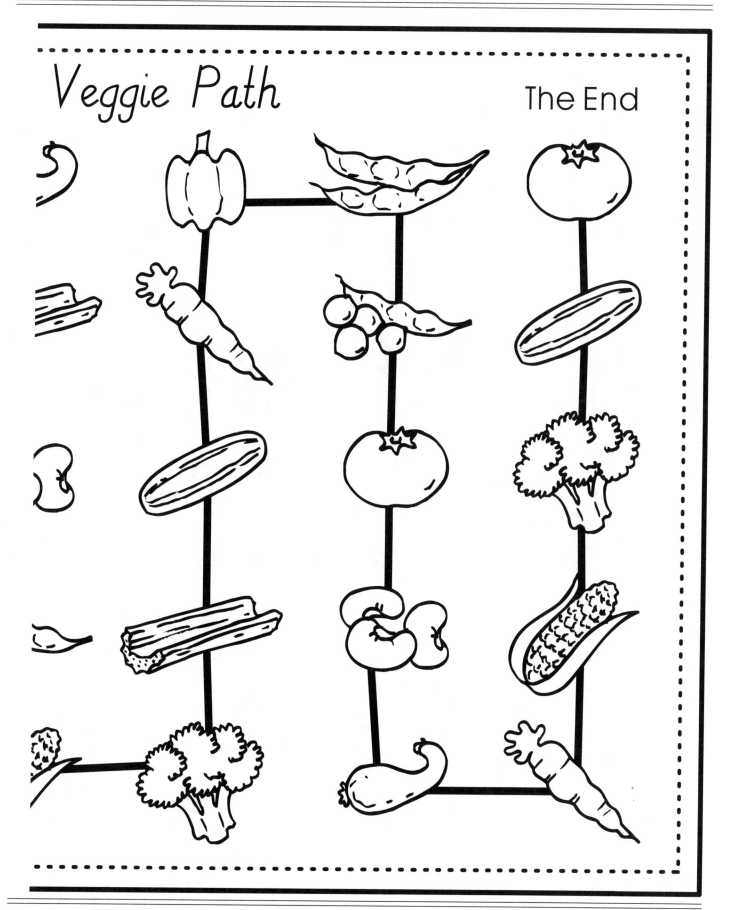

Veggie Path

The End

Follow the Veggie Path Game Cards

green beans

celery

tomato

bell pepper

carrot

squash

corn

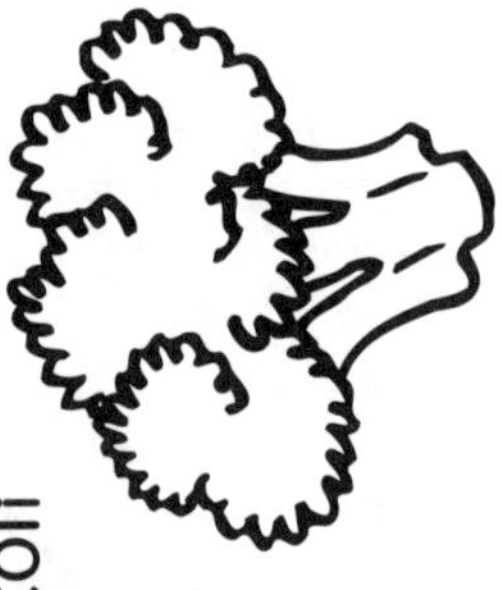

broccoli

cucumber

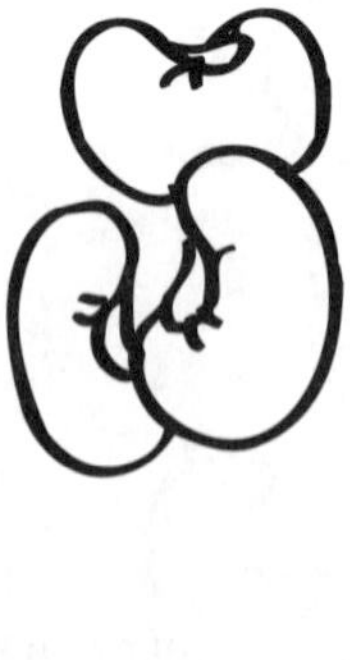

beans

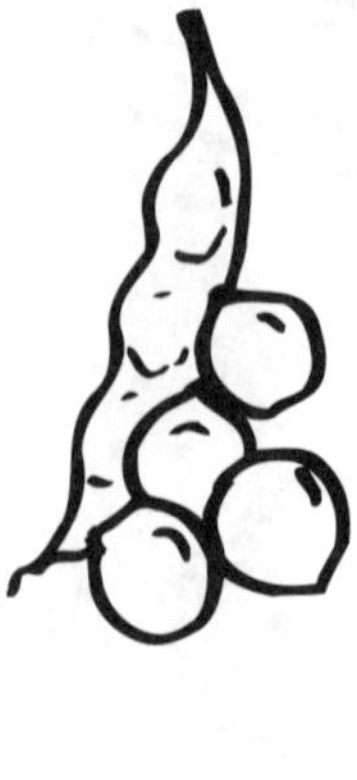

peas

potato

Bug Squares

Provide each child with construction paper squares and ladybugs (p. 34) to color and cut out. Recite oral directions for children to glue ladybugs on construction paper squares. Examples: *Glue the large flying ladybug in the center of a square. Glue three small flying ladybugs on the left side of the large ladybug. Glue seven ladybugs to the back of the square.* When children have completed three squares, help each child tape the squares to a length of yarn to form a Bug Squares mobile.

Ladybugs in My Garden

Provide each child with a sheet of construction paper. Reproduce small ladybugs (p. 34), and a set of garden patterns (p. 37) for children to color and cut. Have children glue the garden patterns along the bottom of construction paper sheets. Then have them glue the ladybugs in their gardens. Invite each child to share his or her garden with the class. Encourage children to tell how many ladybugs are in their gardens; on, under, next to a mushroom, flower pot, leaf, or plant; flying up, down, over, or under a mushroom, flower pot, leaf, or plant.

Ladybugs on Parade

Reproduce gift wrap ladybug bodies and wings for each child. Help children fold and glue wings to the back of each ladybug body. Write each child's initials on the backs of ladybug bodies. Tape a length of fishing line or light-weight yarn to the back of each child's set of ladybugs to form ladybug streamers. Hang the ladybug streamers from the ceiling for a "Ladybugs on Parade" display. Note: Cut gift wrap to standard letter-size sheets to reproduce in a copy machine.

Up, Up, and Away!

Provide each child with a set of flying ladybugs (p. 34) and a landscape pattern (p. 36) to color and cut out. Have children glue their flying ladybugs up in the clouds, on the hot air balloon, or on the kite. Display finished pictures on a bulletin board entitled "Up, Up and Away!"

Ladybugs

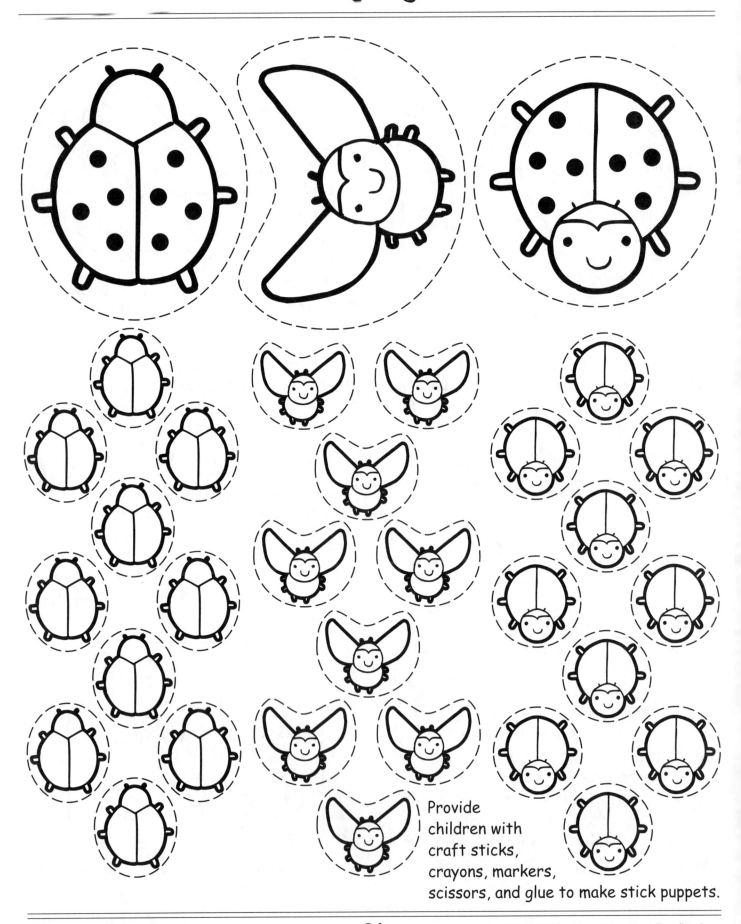

Provide children with craft sticks, crayons, markers, scissors, and glue to make stick puppets.

Ladybug Bodies and Wings

Fold.

Fold.

Fold.

Up, Up and Away Landscape

Garden Patterns

Let's Play *Fly Away Home*

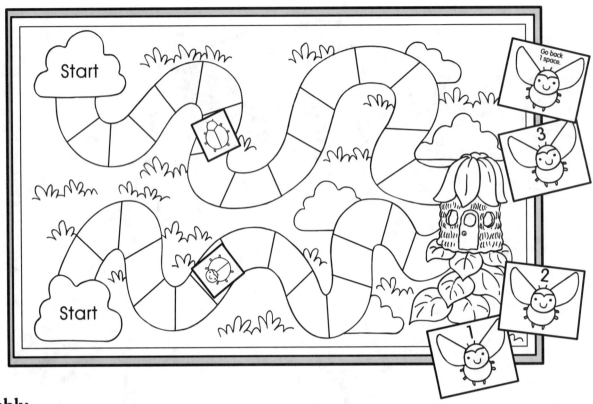

Assembly

Reproduce, color, and cut out the "Fly Away Home" game board patterns. Overlap and match the game board halves at the center. Glue the game board patterns on a sheet of oak tag. Decorate the border around the game board, then laminate. Reproduce, color, laminate, then cut out the pawns and two sets of game cards. Measure, cut, and tape a construction paper pocket to the back of the game board for pawn and game card storage.

To Play

Set up the game board on a table for two players. Shuffle and place the game cards, face down, next to the game board. Each player, in turn, draws a card and moves his or her pawn forward one, two, three spaces, or back one space, as shown on the card. Players place used cards in a discard pile. When all cards have been drawn, reshuffle the discard pile for children to continue playing. Play continues until each ladybug reaches home.

Pawns

Fly Away Home Game Cards

Fly Away Home Game Board

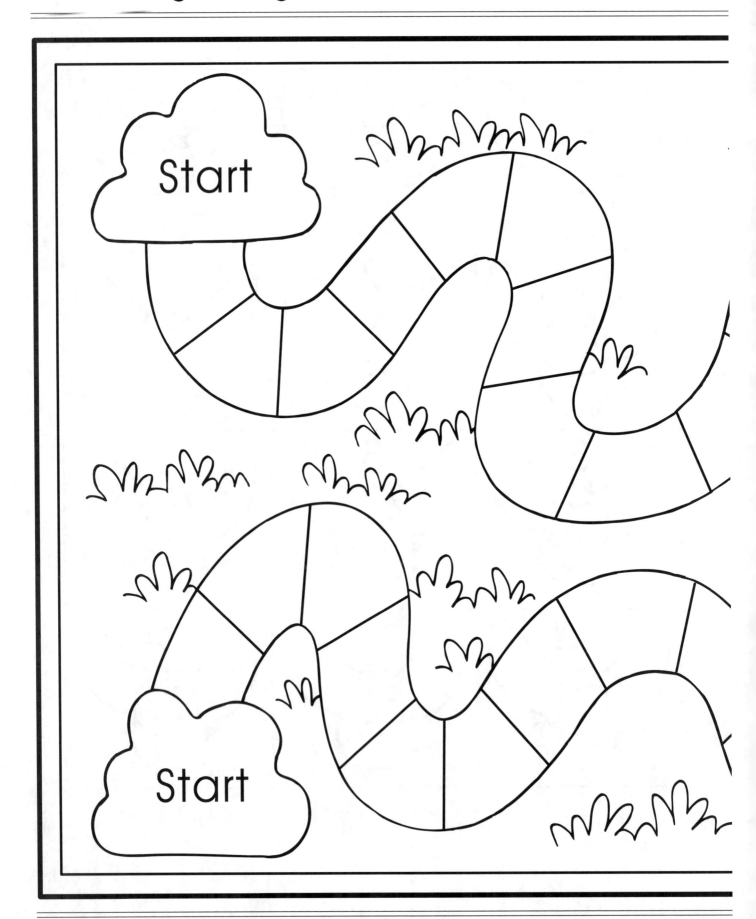

41

Bread Basket Match

Reproduce, color, and cut out three sets of bread loaves and basket patterns (pp. 46-47). Glue a diamond on one set of small, medium, and large bread loaves and baskets. Glue stars, and hearts on the two remaining sets. Write "Bread Basket Match" on a large envelope. Then reproduce, color, cut out, and glue a hen (p. 43) and small bread patterns on the envelope. Store the loaf and basket cutouts in the envelope. Children sort and match the cutouts by size or symbols.

Where's the Little Red Hen?

Decorate the border around a sheet of poster board. Glue 16 Velcro fastener squares (four rows of four) on a sheet of poster board. Enlarge, reproduce, color, laminate, and cut out the Hen and Barnyard Friends (p. 43). Glue a Velcro fastener square to the back of each cutout. Invite children, in turn, to ask "Where's the little red hen?," then place the cutouts on the board according to your answer. Include spatial concepts in your answer. Example: "The little red hen is standing between the duck and the pig."

Barnyard Lotto

Program and reproduce several lotto boards (p. 44) with different combinations of lotto and Free Space cards (p. 45). Reproduce a complete set of cards for each board. Tape an envelope to the back of each board for card storage. Then reproduce and laminate (do not cut apart) one set of lotto cards to use as a "callers sheet." Have each child choose and place a lotto board and cards on his or her desk. Call out "I see a (animal) holding a (shape)." Example: *"I see a hen holding a triangle."* Each child with a match places the matching card on his or her board. Use a wipe-off marker to cross off each card on the callers sheet as it is called. Play continues until all of the children fill their boards. For advanced play, add a board location as follows "I see a hen holding a triangle in the bottom left-hand corner."

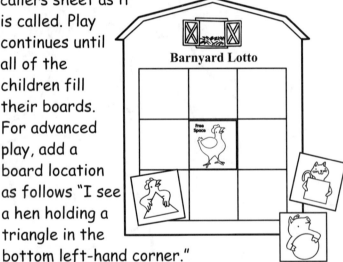

Barnyard Friends Garland

Reproduce hens and baryard friends (p. 43) for children to color and cut out. Tape or staple a length of yarn to the backs of cutouts to form a garland to decorate windows, doors, and display boards.

Hen and Barnyard Friends

Provide children with craft sticks, crayons, markers, scissors, and glue to make stick puppets.

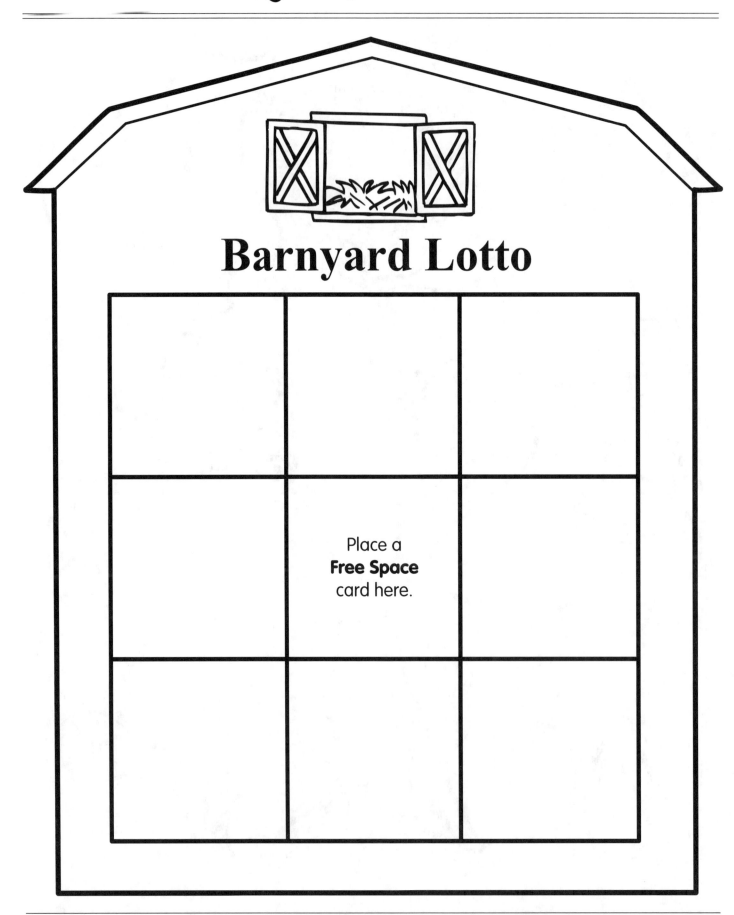

Barnyard Lotto

Place a
Free Space
card here.

Barnyard Lotto Cards

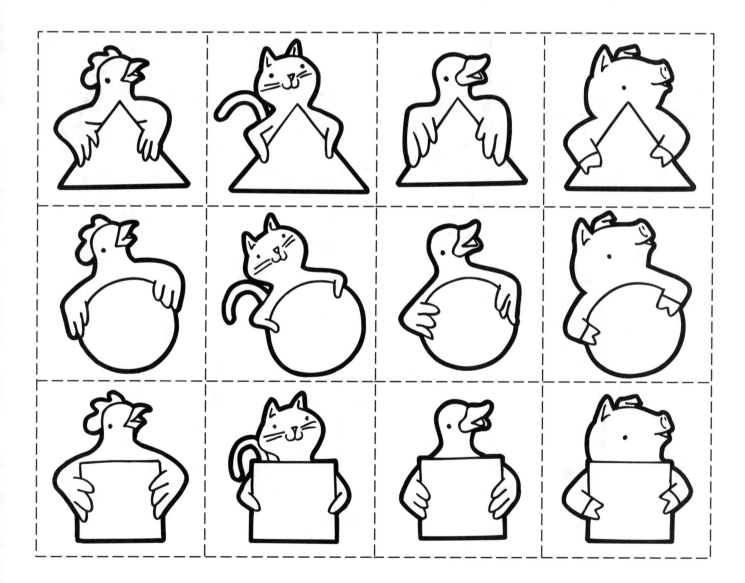

Bread Loaves

Bread Baskets

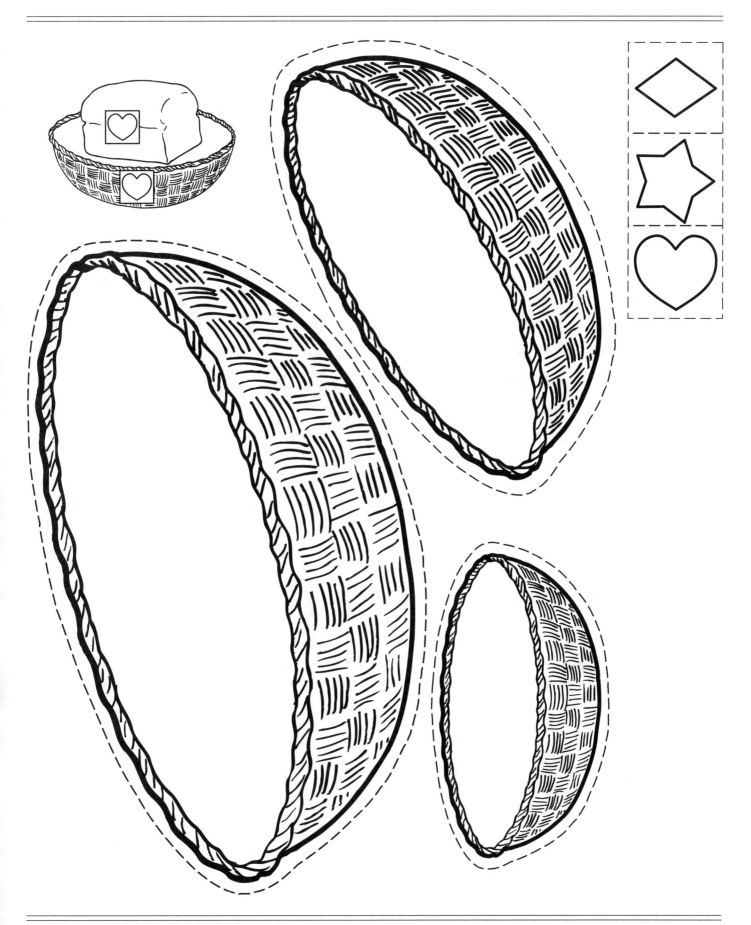

Let's Play *Fill the Bread Basket*

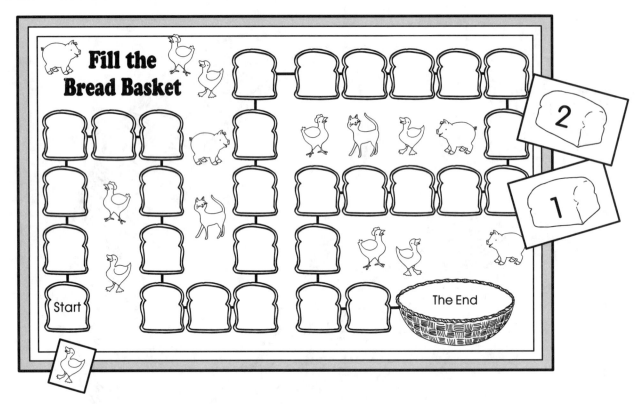

Assembly

Reproduce, color, and cut out the "Fill the Bread Basket" game board patterns. Matching in the center, glue the game board patterns on a sheet of oak tag. Decorate the border around the game board, then laminate. Reproduce, color, laminate, then cut out the pawns and two sets of game cards. Measure, cut, and tape a construction paper pocket to the back of the game board for pawn and game card storage.

To Play

Set up the game board on a table. Shuffle and place the game cards, face down, next to the game board. Each player, in turn, draws a card and moves his or her pawn one or two spaces. Players place used cards in a discard pile. When all cards have been drawn, reshuffle the discard pile for children to continue playing. Play continues until each player reaches the basket at The End.

Pawns

Fill the Bread Basket Game Cards

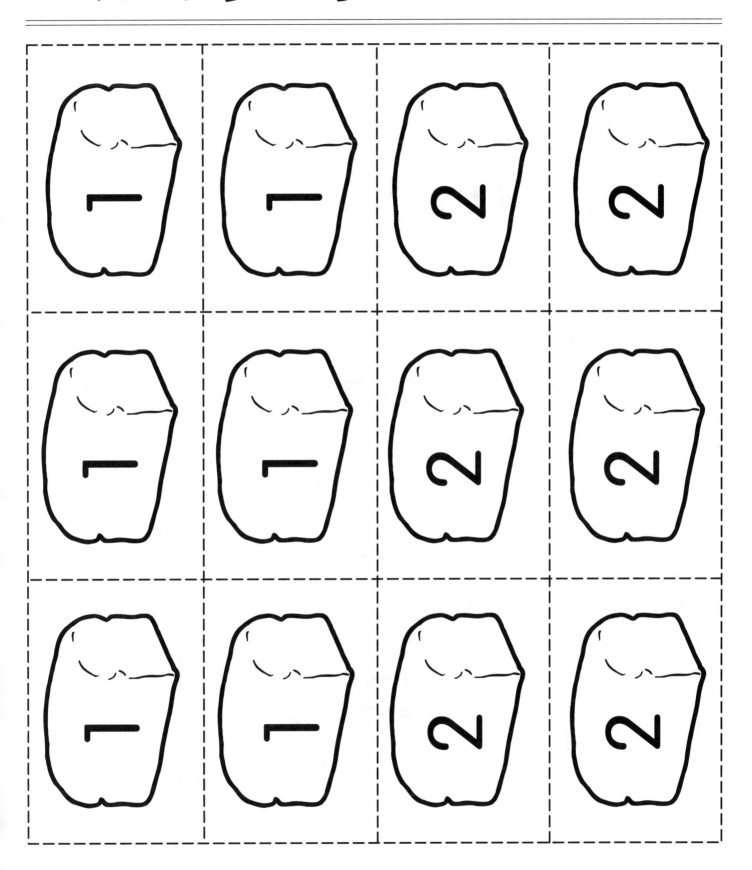

Fill the Bread Basket

Start

Fill the Bread Basket Game Board

The End

After Reading *THE TOWN MOUSE AND THE COUNTRY MOUSE*

Weather Dressing

Prepare a work station with colored chalk, scissors, glue, and construction paper. Have children use chalk to draw three weather landscapes (sunny day, rainy day, cold day). Use hair spray to prevent the chalk from smearing. Then provide children with three town and country mice and one set of clothing patterns (pp. 53-54) to color, cut out, and glue on each appropriate picture. Mice are already wearing sunny day clothing. Have each child dictate a sentence for you to write along the bottom of each picture. Write children's names on the backs of pictures. Display pictures on a bulletin board entitled "Weather Dressing."

All Around Town

Reproduce a set of map patterns (pp. 60-61) for each child to color and cut out. Matching at the center, help children glue the map patterns to the inside of a folder. Write "My Map Folder" on the front of each child's folder. Then have children decorate the front of their folders with town mouse cutouts (p. 53). Glue card storage envelopes to the backs of folders. Reproduce, a set of town cards (p. 58) for children to color and cut apart. Give oral placement instructions for children to place the town cards on the map. Examples: "Place the toy store on the left side of block number three." "Place street light next to the toy store."

Bags Full of Opposites

Prepare a work station with crayons, markers, scissors, and glue. Reproduce 12 shopping bags (p. 55) and one set of opposites cards (pp. 56-57) for children to color and cut out. Have children glue matching sets of opposites cards on each shopping bag. Then help each child stack and staple the bags together to form a booklet.

Country Hide and Seek

Children can use their map folders to play a game of Country Hide and Seek. Reproduce small town and country mice (p. 53) and a set of country cards (p. 59) for each child to color and cut apart. Invite one child at a time to the front of the room. Have the child arrange his or her country patterns on the map, then place each mouse cutout under one of the country patterns. Invite children in turn to ask a question to find where the mice are hiding. Examples: "Is the country mouse hiding in block number one?" "Is the town mouse behind the chicken house?" When both mice are found, another child gets to hide his or her mice.

Town Mouse and Country Mouse

Provide children with craft sticks, crayons, markers, scissors, and glue to make stick puppets.

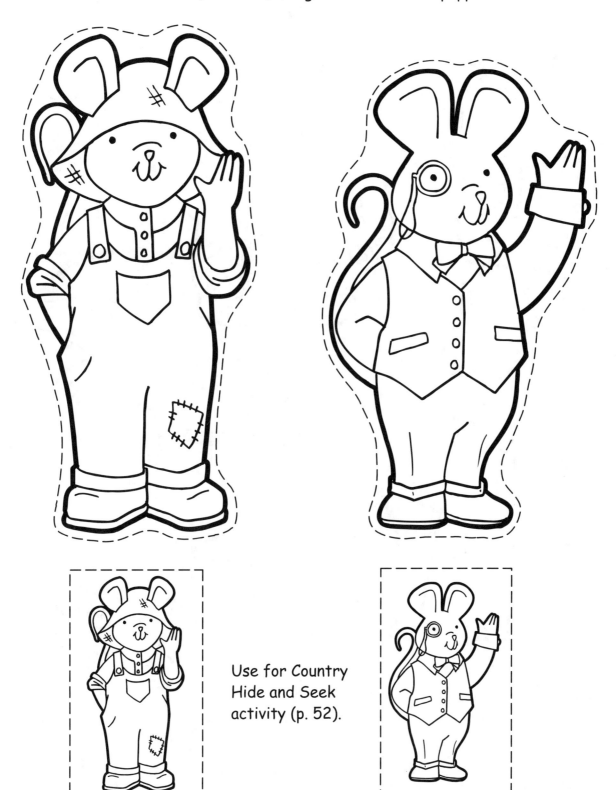

Use for Country Hide and Seek activity (p. 52).

Weather Clothes and Accessories

Shopping Bags

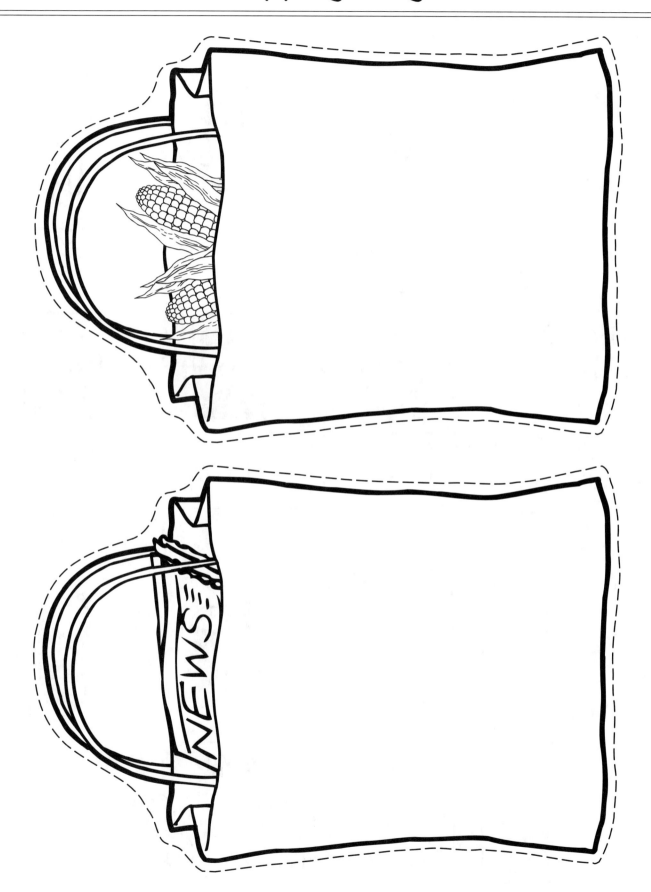

Opposites Cards

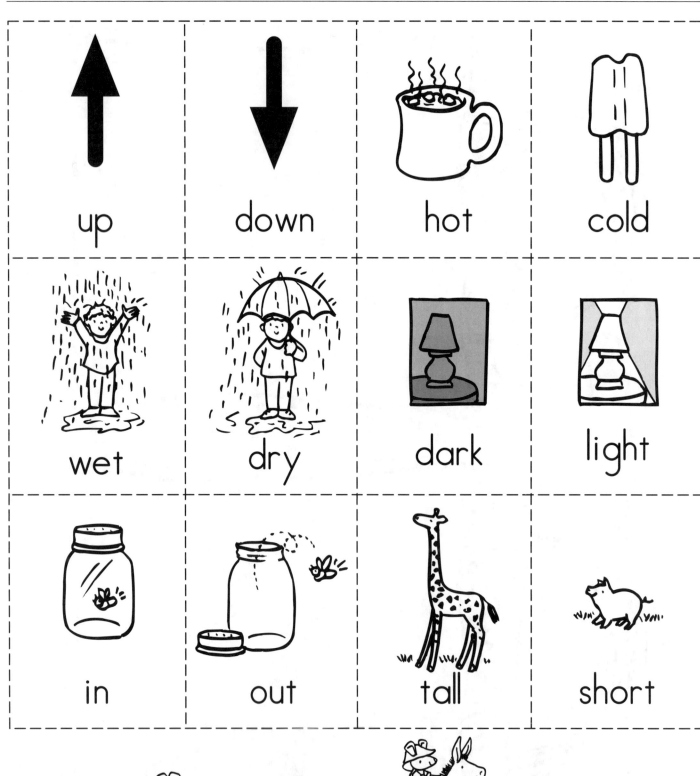

up	down	hot	cold
wet	dry	dark	light
in	out	tall	short

Opposites Cards

near	far	big	little
sweet	sour	soft	hard
left	right	black	white

Town Cards

Stoplight

Street Light

Tree

School

Library

Tree

GROCERY

Grocery Store

Tree

Park

RESTAURANT

Restaurant

HOSPITAL

EMERGENCY

Hospital

Stoplight

Street Light

TOYS

Toy Store

Country Cards

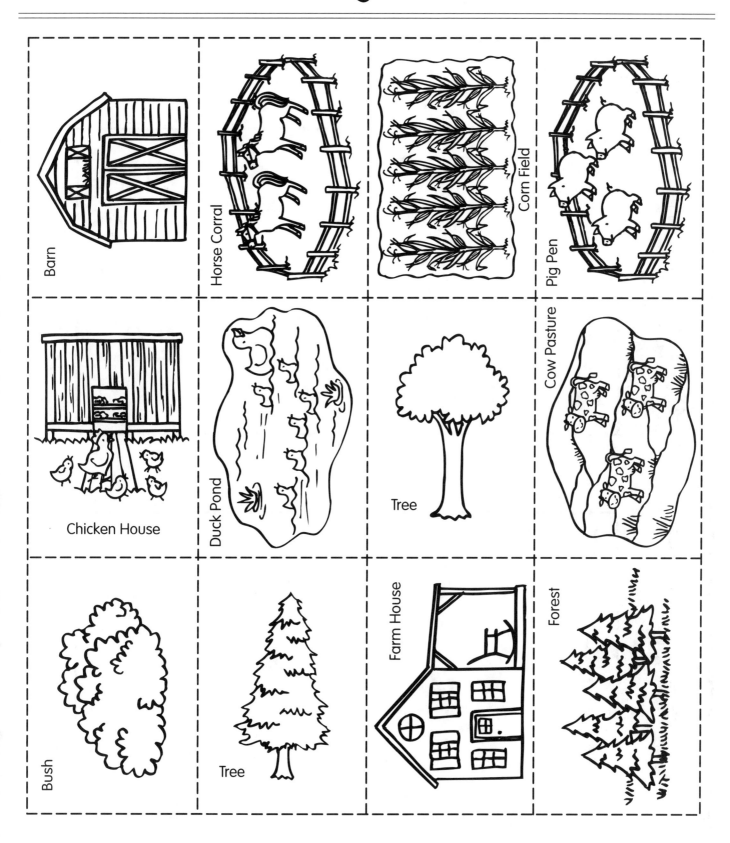

Barn

Horse Corral

Corn Field

Pig Pen

Chicken House

Duck Pond

Tree

Cow Pasture

Bush

Tree

Farm House

Forest

Map

1

3

2

4

Let's Play *A Ride in the Country*

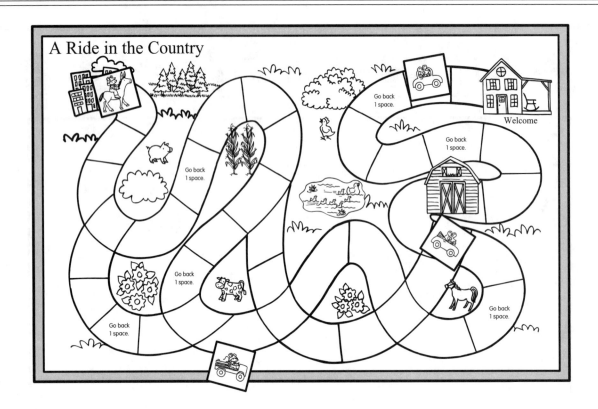

Assembly

Reproduce, color, and cut out the "A Ride in the Country" game board patterns. Overlap and match the game board halves at the center. Glue the game board patterns on a sheet of oak tag. Decorate the border around the game board, then laminate. Reproduce, color, laminate, then cut out the pawns. Tape a small envelope to the back of the game board for pawn storage.

To Play

Set up the game board on a table. Each player, in turn, rolls a die, and moves his or her pawn the matching number of spaces. (Players can take different routes to reach The End.) Play continues until each player reaches the farm house.

Pawns

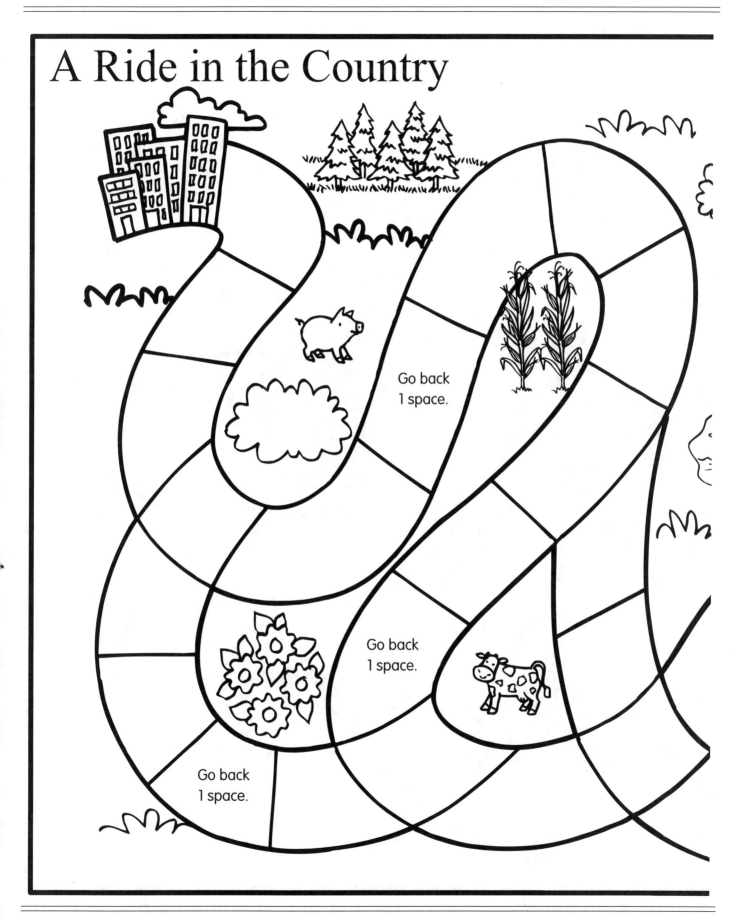

A Ride in the Country

Go back 1 space.

Go back 1 space.

Go back 1 space.

A Ride in the Country Game Board

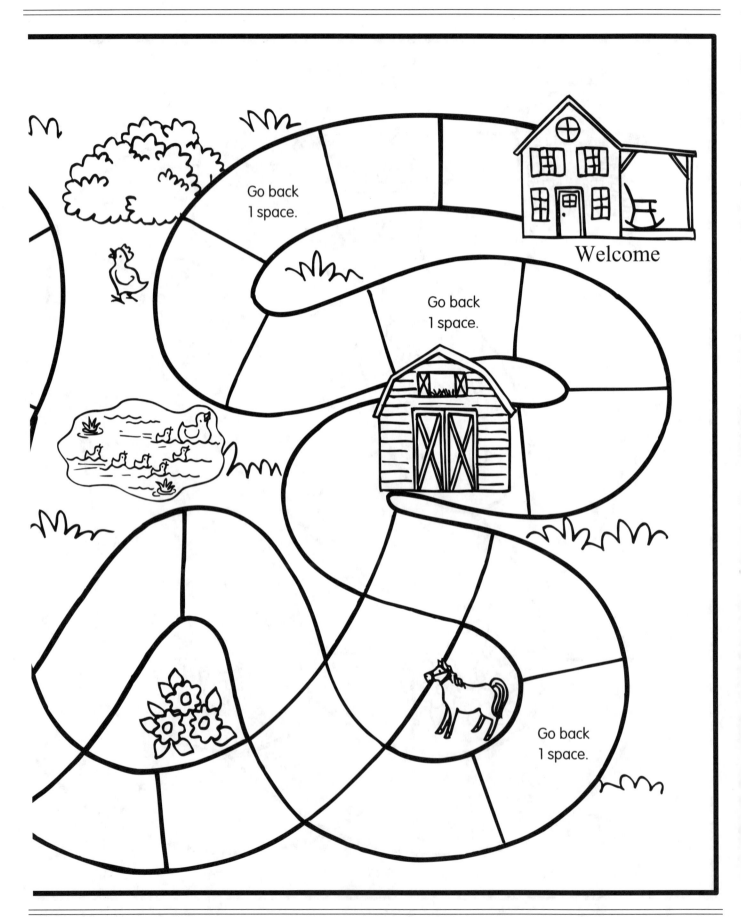

Go back
1 space.

Welcome

Go back
1 space.

Go back
1 space.